Rhymes at Midnight

A New Collection From
Fran Landesman

D1419912

Golden Handshake

First published in 1996 by
Golden Handshake
8 Duncan Terrace
London N1 8BZ

With thanks to Tim Donnelly,
Jane Havell and Jay Landesman

ISBN 0 905150 39 2

SECOND PRINTING 1996

Designed and produced by Jane Havell
Cover design by Richard Gallagher
Printed by The Book Factory, London

Rhymes at Midnight

I play with rhymes at midnight
To fill the quiet hours
Beginning when the movie ends
    Some are puzzles
    Which have no meaning
    And some are friends

They float in from the cosmos
And buzz around my bedroom
Or drop in from the local bars
    Some remind me
    Of lost companions
    And falling stars

Some rhymes settle on the paper
And make themselves at home
Some arrive like nervous strangers
And then become a poem

I hope the day is coming
When we'll forgive each other
For our divided destiny
In the meantime
These rhymes at midnight
    Are yours
    With love
      From me

By the Same Author

The Ballad of the Sad Young Men and Other Verse,
  Polytantric Press, 1975
Invade My Privacy, Jonathan Cape, 1978
More Truth Than Poetry, The Permanent Press, 1979
Is It Overcrowded in Heaven?, Golden Handshake, 1981
The Thorny Side of Love, sun tavern fields, 1992

FRAN LANDESMAN, born in Manhattan, has lived in
London for thirty years and has been writing since the
1950s. Her experiences with Jack Kerouac, John Clellon
Holmes and G. Legman inspired her lyrics for *The
Nervous Set,* the first cool jazz musical on Broadway,
which opened in 1959. She has penned songs with
Tommy Wolf which have entered the popular music
canon, including *Spring Can Really Hang You Up the Most*
and *Ballad of the Sad Young Men.* Regarded by many as
the singer's songwriter, her lyrics have provided
material for Barbra Streisand, Ella Fitzgerald, Mabel
Mercer, Bette Midler, Tony Bennett, Shirley Bassey and
scores of others whose recordings of them have sold
millions.

Stage productions of her work include *Loose
Connections, Invade My Privacy, Confessions of a Middle-
Aged Juvenile Delinquent* in London's West End, and *The
Decline of the Middle West* Off-Broadway. *There's
Something Irresistible in Down,* with music by Simon
Wallace and played by actors from the Royal Shakespeare
Company, was performed in London's Young Vic Theatre
in 1996.

Fran Landesman is a frequent broadcaster on BBC
radio and is planning a concert tour in 1997. She lives in
Islington, north London, and has two sons, one grand-
child and her husband, author Jay Landesman.

Contents

DARK CLOUDS

FACES AND FANCIES

ON LOCATION

EDUCATED GUESSES

REMIND ME

REMIND me that it doesn't matter
Remind me that the world won't stop
Remind me that we'll go on living
Even if the show's a flop

Remind me not to be so solemn
And tell me that it's just a game
Remind me that it doesn't matter
While making one more grab for fame

We won't discuss what happens next
Or 'What's it all about?'
One day you walked into my life
One day you'll wander out

Remind me there will still be music
No matter how the story ends
Remind me that it doesn't matter
And you and I will stay good friends

You'll Believe Anything

She tells you that she's fascinated
By your person and your attributes
She says of all the guys she's dated
There's not one that's even half so cute

If you believe that, you'll believe anything
You'll believe that Elvis is alive and well
   And still the king
You'll believe there's nothing wrong
   With getting fat
You'll believe anything if you believe that

If you believe that, you'll believe the TV ads
You'll believe prosperity and jobs are there
   For college grads
You'll believe the one you love
   Can't leave you flat
You'll believe anything if you believe that

I hate to to be the one who mentions
That the girl you worship thinks you're a fool
You're buying all her wild inventions
Even if she tells you that pigs shoot pool

If you believe that, you'll believe in Church and State
You'll believe there really is a chance you'll fill
   An inside straight
You'll believe too much cocaine
   Can't kill a cat
You'll believe anything if you believe that

If You're Doing It Right

ALL that groaning and lusting
And oozing and thrusting
And screwing all night
Sex is simply disgusting
If you're doing it right

All the oiling and soaping
And poking and groping
And moans of delight
Sex is better than doping
If you're doing it right

If you're doing it right it's dark and forbidden
If you're doing it right you must keep it hidden
Drag it out in the light? You gotta be kiddin'
Sex ought to be mean
Not cheerful and clean

Sex is sweaty and hurty
And sticky and spurty
Keep it well out of sight
Sex has gotta be dirty
If you're doing it right

THERAPY

Is the latest instalment of your personal soap
    Depressing you?
Do you feel like summer will never be the same?
Do you hide a yawn when your Romeo starts
    Undressing you?
Do you dream of someone new and feel ashamed?

Have you been in therapy? Would you like to try?
Peel away the outer you. Have a little cry.
Therapy can prop you up when you're on the brink
Tell the secrets of your soul to a licensed shrink

Are your children a problem? Are they dirty and deaf
    To your requests?
Do you sit and dream of how sweet life used to be?
Do you choke back the anger? Do you wish you could get
    It off your chest?
Have you lost your grip on what's called reality?

Iron out those little kinks
Schitz or paranoid
You can be a smoother you
Thanks to Dr Freud

Had it not been for therapy
I might have saved some dough
But I'd have jumped off Tower Bridge
Many years ago

THE ABSENCE OF A DESIGNER

WHEN science says something
That seems to deny
The existence of the great creator
Why is there such an outcry?
Why do we hanker
For a Daddy in the sky?
Isn't what *is* good enough?
The blossoms and the blizzards
The humans and their children
The furry animals and lazy lizards
The oceans dancing in the light
Full of amazing fish
Aren't they enough?
Sometimes the fish look so stylish
It's hard to banish
The notion of a divine designer
But if he isn't there
Must we care?
Does the absence of a designer
Diminish the glamour of the lion?
Anyway, it's a beautiful creation
And if God made it
She deserves congratulations

CANNABIS

You can drink champagne till you're down the drain
All the gourmets idolize it
Though fermented grain often rots the brain
All the better people prize it
At a football game boozers stab and maim
But they don't illegalize it
Supermarket sweets sold as children's treats
Rot their teeth and who denies it

Now I sure would miss my cannabis
Though it's risky when you buys it
'Cause the boys in blue they will hassle you
If they identifies it
And some day, alas, they may bust my ass
Will I quit? Why, you must be joking
As you raise your glass you can bet your brass
I'm gonna go on smoking

NOTHING LASTS FOREVER

NOTHING lasts forever
Not sand, not sea, not stars
Not candles or convictions
And not this love of ours

Nothing lasts forever
Not fire nor ice-cream
Not hope, nor heat, nor hunger
And surely not this dream

Yes, my darling, that's the sad news
That's the good news *and* the bad news
The darkest night, the dullest day
Will ultimately pass away

Nothing lasts forever
We're changing as I speak
The worm of time is feeding
Upon your tender cheek

As this delightful moment
Recedes into the past
A part of its perfection
Is that it cannot last

FORBIDDEN GAMES

FORBIDDEN games are for the brave
For boys and girls who travel light
Without a face they have to save
Or cases labelled 'wrong' and 'right'

Forbidden games are hard to beat
Especially when they're played with skill
Forbidden fruit is twice as sweet
Until you have to pay the bill

Scientists flirt with destruction
Their games may blow us away
I've got a taste for seduction
What sort of games do you play?

We never question if it's worth
The price of our forbidden joys
Forbidden games can cost the earth
But people love expensive toys

LET'S NOT THINK ABOUT THAT

YOUR overtures overjoy me
The hand you're holding is pat
I know you're going to destroy me
But let's not think about that

Let's open up to each other
And see if sex can be fun
Try not to think of your mother
And I won't think of my son

We've got a little spare time
We like each other's looks
And we can have a rare time
Forget about the hooks

Just go ahead and enjoy me
I'll play the mouse to your cat
I know you're going to destroy me
But let's not think about that

OTHER PEOPLE'S PLATES

How appetising is the food
On other people's plates
The scent of other people's loves
And other people's hates

How pleasurable it is to dress
In other people's clothes
To step inside their shoes and see
Just how their garden grows

It's fun to nibble at other lives
To try their husbands and taste their wives
Their grass is greener, their rose more red
The sex is keener
In someone else's bed

I just can't wait to read your book
Until at last it's mine
Somehow the thing that I possess
Is always less divine

A little distance lends such charm
When eyeing other mates
How appetising is the food
On other people's plates

THE SECRET OF SILENCE

I wish you would teach me the secret of silence
I wish you would show me the way to be still
My thoughts keep on flying in different directions
My words simply clutter the spaces they fill

I know that the spaces are really important
You needn't convince me that less can be more
I'm trying to choke back the words that I utter
I hear them with horror as onward they pour

I want to be imperious
And speak in whispers all men obey
I want to be mysterious
But I keep giving myself away

I'm sure I'd do better to play Mona Lisa
Seductively smiling whenever you're here
I know that you're weary of these revelations
Relentlessly beating a path to your ear

My insides escape in a terrible torrent
Or else I'm a prisoner inside a black hole
I wish you would teach me the secret of silence
That isn't a sulk or a pain in the soul

A Message from the Management

The management cannot accept
Responsibility
For umbrellas, morals, hats or hearts
Elation or ennui

If the customers forget themselves
And heads begin to spin
We can't guarantee you'll go away
The way that you came in

Don't spill the secrets of your life
Don't show your hand or bare your soul
When speaking of the job or wife
Please use a little self-control

If you go ahead and drink your fill
You may set your fancy free
You may fall into a lover's eyes
Or discover someone's knee

If you leave behind your moral code
Or lose your dignity
The management cannot accept
Responsibility

For the New Recruit

It makes me sick
When I think what life will do to you
'No,' you say, 'I'm an optimist.'
You outline your plan of attack
It's my banner you will carry into battle
But I remember other eyes
That shone as yours do now
One day they all stumble and fall
On the rocks of reality
It was never my fault
I was merely part of the process
Of growing up

SELLING OUR SECRETS

WE'RE all selling our secrets
Trying to gain some visibility
Grabbing a handle on celebrity
We're telling our tales

We're all selling our stories
Making the most out of a love affair
Laying the seamy inner landscape bare
We're making some sales

What the great man said, how he was in bed
With a picture spread
So we turn a trick – we're just doing *schtic*
Till they make the flick

We're all spelling it right out
Stripping the attics of our private lives
Stories of buggery and murdered wives
The sex, the star trips, the scenes
    Selling our secrets
    Selling our dreams

We've got stuff to sell from the private hell
Of the author's youth
For quite modest fees we help Ph.D.s
In their search for truth

We're all tearing our clothes off
Flashing our assets for the gutter press
Out of the closet with the bloody mess
    We're naming the name
    Feeling no shame
    Selling our secrets

THAT'S WHAT THEY TOLD ME

THAT'S a leaf, they told me
That's a cat and that's a star
Eat up all your salad
What a silly girl you are

That's your school, they told me
That's your teacher. That's your seat
Try to be like Carole
She's so pretty. She's so sweet

What's wrong with you?
You're not really trying
You're always in a dream
Your work is poor
Now why are you crying?
You'll never make the team

If we scare and scold you
That's because we care so much
This is love, they told me
Now grow up and keep in touch

BE UNPREPARED!

I'M always getting ready for the big event
Imagining the outcome, picturing the scene
I know I ought to take life as it comes along
But I am too familiar with how things go wrong
    I wish I didn't feel so scared
    It's better to be unprepared

I wish I didn't know about the big, bad world
Remembering the flim-flam, dreaming of the burn
I know my season in the sun won't last for long
But maybe someone wonderful will love my song
    I wish I didn't feel so scared
    It's better to be unprepared

I'd like to loosen up and play it all by ear
Listen to the music, do my little dance
I wish I didn't know the way the movie ends
Go on sweetheart, surprise me and we'll still be friends
    It's better to be unprepared
    I wish I didn't feel so scared

SUCCESS

I've heard fame is better avoided
And success lets you down with a bang
I've had a small taste and enjoyed it
So I questioned my friend Dr Laing

I asked if his fame had destroyed him
He wouldn't admit that it had
I asked if the spotlight annoyed him
He said that it wasn't so bad

'Success is a great consolation,'
Said the mythical R. D. Laing
In the midst of our black desolation
It reminds us that once we sang

Success is a key in your pocket
Or it may be a stone in your shoe
But I really don't think you should knock it
Until it has happened to you

ARE YOU SATISFIED?

DOES the life you're living seem a little dry
Are you disappointed with your piece of pie
Do you think you should have made a better score
Are you satisfied with what you settled for?

Do you get up early just to walk the dog
Have you started praying? Do you dance or jog?
Do you worry much about the Third World War
Are you satisfied with what you settled for?

Maybe it's time to make your mind up
Maybe your time is running out
Will you be asking as you wind up
Just what the fuss was all about?

When the two of you are side by side in bed
Do you ever wonder what is in her head
Do you think of knocking at another door
Are you satisfied with what you settled for?

Are you sick and tired of the same old scene
Has domestic bliss become a dull routine
Have you had enough or do you want some more
Are you satisfied with what you settled for?

Silver Linings

Weather Report

There's a slow-moving depression
At the bottom of my heart
There's a lack of any action
In my love life or my art

There's no way that I can shift them
Dark clouds follow me like pets
When I drag myself to parties
I just bump into regrets

But life goes on. The wheel goes round
The winners lose. The lost are found
Some day my turn will come around

That old weatherman keeps saying
There's a high just round the bend
And that villain in the corner
Could turn out to be a friend

He will ask me what I'm drinking
And his eyes will shine for me
And my slow-moving depression
Will drift slowly out to sea

BEHIND THE TIMES

THEY sip their coffee and read the papers
In a shabby café, lovers past their prime
He's raised the pages to hide their faces
As they steal a little kiss behind *The Times*

Their clothes aren't trendy but they're contented
They both enjoy their routines and their rhymes
They're a bit old-fashioned but they've decided
That it's not so bad to be behind the times

Once their games and their gossip
Were the state of the art
But time plays funny tricks
Now they laugh at the system
As it falls apart
And pray they won't get sick

They sip their coffee and read the papers
And shudder at contemporary crimes
They love each other's familiar faces
So they rise above the temper of the times

As they steal a little kiss
Behind *The Times*

Nuts to 'The Real Thing'

I don't want the real thing
I want to be with you
I don't want forever
This afternoon will do

Go ahead and fool me
You do it awfully well
Being here is heaven
Reality is hell

It's paying bills and where you put your toothbrush
It's Ma and Pa and picking up your clothes
While you and I are killing time together
It doesn't matter how the garden grows

Monday has been cancelled
Reality is out
There isn't any future
So let's just mess about

This is like the movies
Too lovely to be true
I don't want the real thing
I want to be with you

CRAZY DAYS

Do you feel shy and out of step
Invisible in school or pub?
If you're not any average kid
It's time to join the Crazy Club

Encourage people close to you
Your best friend, pussy cat or wife
To do a crazy deed a day
And lead the crazy way of life

Walk backward every chance you get
And eat your dinner upside down
Wear skirts or trousers inside out
And somersault around the town

Be strange, be weird at work and play
(Except when handling a knife)
Make all your crazy dreams come true
And lead the crazy way of life

CHORUS
Crazy pets, crazy plays
Going through a crazy phase
Crazy walks, crazy ways
We enjoy these crazy days

The Profits of Pain

We've made necklaces of notes and words that glitter
We've collected gems and polished them for years
So the world can see how beautifully we suffer
And reward us for the products of our tears

We have woven broken dreams into tiaras
Disappointment and despair have made them strong
We did not omit the love scenes and the laughter
But those moments never lasted very long

We've made lyrics out of joy and desolation
Fashioned poetry and music from the heart
We've displayed our tender moods and our emotions
And the furies that were tearing us apart

We have mined the darkest moments of our nightmares
And we hope these sacrifices aren't in vain
For the world must see how beautifully we suffer
And reward us for the products of our pain

On Ageing

Ancient lady bravely
Zipping through the traffic
Heading into winter
On your battered bicycle
How you lift my heart with hope
    That I too
May grow old heroically
    Like you

THE ICE DANCERS

LIKE animated china figurines
The ice dancers glide into our hearts
Exquisite parodies of sexuality
Without struggle or strain
This is how love ought to be
All the parts
Flowing in perfect synchronicity
Pain-free and clean
No one can fault Torvill and Dean
Except some feminist
Longing for the day when she
Tosses him over her shoulder
Whirling him into the ultimate dip
And the final frozen delight

HAPPY NEW YEAR

I'M feeling cool and collected
Facing another New Year
All of the prospects are pleasing
Skies are beginning to clear

Maybe I miss you a little
Maybe I wish you were here
Still I'm not wasting my chances
Waiting for you to appear

You were my fantasy lover
You were the thorn in my side
Now that such pleasures are over
Thanks for a wonderful ride

Sometimes I'll catch myself sighing
Saying your name with a curse
Still I've got one consolation
Your headache's bound to be worse

Really I'm feeling much better
I've shed my last bitter tear
And though I don't fancy your chances
I wish you a happy New Year

ART AS CATHARSIS

I'VE worked out a method of dealing
With traumas afflicting the heart
By making the pain into patterns
And turning the ache into art

Whenever a lover betrays me
Or living seems less then sublime
I don't feel the time has been wasted
I pour it all into a rhyme

This isn't the perfect solution
But still it's a fair stratagem
And people who read what I've written
May feel that I've spoken for them

So now it's goodbye to you darling
I know that it's all going wrong
But I can make use of the heartache
By putting it into a song

A TOAST (OR GOOD WISHES)

HERE'S pearls in your oyster
And plums in your pie
Here's fun in your future
And stars in your sky

Here's mail in your mailbox
Here's wisdom and wealth
Here's sun in your summer
Good luck and good health

Here's everything you wish yourself
May all your dreams be sweet
Here's wine and whisky on your shelf
And wings upon your feet

Here's fruit in your garden
And cash in your hand
A lover to meet you
Wherever you land

Here's strength to your elbow
Success in your art
Here's pearls in your oyster
And me in your heart

THE IRRITATED OYSTER

THE howl of the unassuaged ego
Is a terrible strain on the ear
And your story of pain and betrayal
Is a tale no one's eager to hear
But at least there is one consolation
For a bruised or abused boy or girl
Affliction is fuel for an artist
One day you may bring forth a pearl

What if you're underrated
Heartbroken and deflated
Only the irritated
Oyster makes the pearl

An oyster to be a producer
Must swallow a morsel of sand
Which causes severe irritation
And slowly begins to expand
The oyster will sit there and suffer
Though its neighbours may call it a churl
For it knows at the end of its labour
It will open, and voilà – a pearl!

So if you're suffocated
Bitter and badly mated
As we've already stated
You will be celebrated
Only the irritated
Oyster makes the pearl

Dark Clouds

Goodbye To All That

Goodbye days of jazz and joking
Goodbye booze and food that's fried
Goodbye glamour, so long smoking
Hello thoughts of suicide

Farewell days of fun and flirting
So long sex – so glad we came
Now there's always something hurting
Hello specs and walking frame

So long lovely finger-lickers
Goodbye life that late we led
Hello cramps and dodgy tickers
Soon we'll be the grateful dead

Goodbye Ronnie, goodbye Lenny
Goodbye pretty girls and boys
Got to go and spend a penny
Hello geriatric joys

HARD TIMES ON EASY STREET

HARD times on Easy Street
The Prince kicks Cinderella
Wakes up on Queasy Street
A most unhappy fella

Wise guys are goin' bust
Pride takes a tumble
Who can you really trust?
Ex-models mumble

No one to lick your feet
Your lover's on the run now
Toy boys can't stand the heat
The nightlife isn't fun now

Kisses are not so sweet
Assets are frozen
Bad news on Easy Street
Hell for the chosen

CHORUS
Hard times on Easy Street
Blood on the balance sheet
Death to a disco beat
Hard times on Easy Street

Fear stalks a shadow land
Where futures looked so golden
Now who can understand
The world we're growing old in?

Nothing is what it seemed
Heroes are humbled
All the big dreams we dreamed
Faded and crumbled

And it's –
Hard times on Easy Street
Blood on the balance sheet
Death to a disco beat
Hard times on Easy Street

THE SILENCE

WE punish each other with our silence
Punctuated by sighs
We push and shove each other
With our silence
More eloquent than the sonnets of Shakespeare
We save our sweet talk for strangers
When we speak
Anger pursues us like a school of sharks
We dance gracefully
Till a sudden fin breaks the surface
Rage boils up in our throats
And the thirst for blood
Who can remember why?
We are both killers
   But without you
    I would die

THE LOSER

ALL that I could lose I lost
Never stopped to count the cost
Keys and wallets, coats and gloves
Glasses, tickets, lighters, loves

Lost them laughing after school
Left them at the swimming pool
Lost my hankies, handbags, books
Lost my memory and my looks

Lost my Mama's emerald ring
Lost my castle and my king
Didn't know what they were worth
Nowadays they cost the earth

What a careless girl was I
Taking chances, getting high
Never stopped to count the cost
All that I could lose I lost

Lost my way and lost my head . . .
Where was I? . . . I've lost the thread

You Can't Take Yes

You can't take yes for an answer
Affection makes you fall apart
If I'd known that when I met you
I'd have saved myself a wounded heart

You tried so hard to entrap me
While I was playing hard to get
When I go half way to meet you
You act as though we've never met

A moment of emotion
Seems to give you a scare
It makes you feel embarrassed
When I show that I care

Though we've had good times together
You really are an awful mess
You keep on asking the question
But you don't know how to take a yes

CRY OF THE UNPUBLISHED POET

WHY did they print that poem?
That's what we must discover
Why those words in that order?
Who is it speaking to?
What does it seek to do?
It's not speaking to me
It has no melody
No shape that I can see
It's the sort of poem
That makes people think
They don't like poetry
It has no beat, no meat
And no wine
Why, oh why
Didn't they print mine?

BUSTING OUR ASSES GRATIS

Busting our asses gratis
That's all we seem to do
Some people hit the jackpot
That's not for me and you

Playing at someone's party
Writing a song on spec
Life is one long audition
Here on the lower deck

The money is an insult
When we get a paying gig
I wish that I could pass out
And wake up to find we're big

How do we keep on going
It's getting hard to take
Busting our asses gratis
When do we get a break?

It's Your Funeral

I used to fantasise that when I died
Everyone who knew me would be ruby-eyed
Weeping for the person so few appreciated
Mourning for the poet so sorely underrated

But now atomic menace grows and threats proliferate
The world may be too dark a place to care about my fate
Gone are my dreams of flattering attention from posterity
Collected bits of me won't rest in any university

There won't be time to peruse my work
    In creative writing classes
When the few survivors try to save
    Their radioactive asses
My private parts and poems will blaze
Without a tear or word of praise

Who will lie on quilted satin
With their hair discreetly curled
When the undertaker's busy
At the funeral of the world?

THE LIVING DEAD

THE dead live a long, long time
We carry them in our hearts
Groaning beneath their weight
Their words and arresting faces
Follow us in our dreams
Crying 'Too late! Too late!'

JEWISH HAIKU

THAT summer I met a handsome biker on crutches
'Everybody's got a brick wall
Waiting for them somewhere'
He said, smiling

FACES AND FANCIES

ALL MOUTH AND NO TROUSERS

YOU'RE all mouth and no trousers
You're all sauce and no steak
You're all hat and no cattle
    Gimme a break

You're all eyes and no stomach
You're all crust and no pie
You're all talk and no music
    You never try

You make a wonderful first impression
From a distance you look hot
But those who stick around soon discover
All the stuff you haven't got

You're all style and no content
You're all duck and no punch –
But you're here and I'm hungry
    Let's have lunch?

THE LAST SMOKER

THE last smoker
Stares hopelessly out at the rain
The last smoker
Is searching his pockets in vain

The smoke police are closing in
Their sniffers never fail
If they detect a whiff of smoke
The culprit goes to jail

The new people
Are clean-living, God-fearing folk
They drink nothing
That's stronger than Diet Coke

They want to build a better world
They haven't time to kid
They'd be ashamed to misbehave
The way their parents did

The last smoker
Has taken his final toke
He'll soon be dead and buried
Along with the very last joke

Gone are the Lucky Strikes
That lovers shared
Lost are our liberties
In the land of the banned
And the home of the scared

HELL'S ANGEL

You walked into my dream last night
And made yourself at home
You asked if you could have a bath
And could you use my comb

Your hung your halo on the door
And folded up your wings
As though you'd never been away
You rummaged through my things

You brushed some stardust off your sleeve
And danced around the room
You said that you'd come back to bring
A message from the tomb

You said that you'd been playing in
The rock band in the sky
With Jimi, John and Mama Cass
And all of them could fly

And everything was right as rain
And all our friends were swell
And one day we would meet again
In what some fools call hell

How's Never For You?

Although I may seem free
From your point of view
Thursday's no good for me
How's never for you?

I don't need company
My doctor is due
Thursday's no good for me
How's never for you?

My schedule is full I fear
I'm anxious and depressed
I'd rather you remembered me
When I was at my best

Friday is booked I see
And Saturday too
Sunday's no good for me
How's never for you?

What made you want to get in touch?
It took a lot of nerve
But even if I had the time
What purpose would it serve?

It's brave of you to call
Right out of the blue
Thursday's no good at all
How's never for you?

HYDE AND SEEK

LET me see your Mr Hyde side
The side you hide from me
Up till now you've only shown me
How charming you can be

Dr Jekyll, I adore you
I have no complaint
But how long can you continue
Acting like a saint?

Underneath your sunny surface
Some darkness must exist
Or you wouldn't be quite human
The plot would have no twist

You won't lose me, Dr Jekyll
If you let me peek
We could come a little closer
Playing Hyde and seek

We can never stick together
And stay starry-eyed
I'm in love with Dr Jekyll
Now show me Mr Hyde

DON'T CHANGE

Don't change
Stay the way that you are
Don't change
You were always a star
It's wonderful the way you hold up
When others are beginning to get fat
When everybody else has sold up
You'll still be pulling rabbits from your hat

So cheers!
I'm still mad for your face
The years
Only add to your grace
It's marvellous to see you coming
Arrayed in splendour, cheering up the street
A Jewish prince who's done a little slumming
Like Fred Astaire you never miss a beat

Don't leave
For the world that's so wide
I'd grieve
Without you by my side
Time marches on but you're still dancing
Still trying to extend your range
Technology may keep advancing
And things and people grow more strange

But please don't go too far
Just stay the way you are
Don't change

FOR A TROUBADOUR

Just think of what you might have been
You could have studied biz. admin.
Or marketing or dentistry
Instead of rhyme and melody
But something turned your youthful feet
Toward music and the swinging street
The house of cards where dreamers wake
And break their hearts to get a break

You might have been an engineer
A decent, sober, safe career
And married well (well, more or less)
Instead of living in a mess
You don't make much to put away
Against that famous rainy day
You should have found a helpful mate
To push you on and share your fate

But something turned your youthful feet
Toward music and the swinging street
The house of cards where dreamers wake
In some strange bed they didn't make
My brave and battered harlequin
You should have studied biz. admin.
Instead of living dangerously
And making songs for fools like me

DID WE HAVE A GOOD TIME?

WOULD you please get me a drink
Could you turn off the sun
Who are you? Where did we meet?
Did we have any fun?

I don't know how I got here
From the scene of the crime
Who am I? Where have I been?
Did I have a good time?

I really want to thank you
For putting up with me
I won't have any breakfast
Well, just a cup of tea

Why am I wearing your shirt?
I don't feel very fine
You're so kind. Why do you smile?
Did you have a good time?

It's awfully nice to meet you
I hope we'll keep in touch
But I'm afraid my memory
Just isn't up to much

How would you sum up last night?
Was it blah or sublime?
What was true? What did we do?
Did we have a good time?

QUID PRO QUO

DON'T want to hog the conversation
Like the rest of the bores
But will you listen to my story
If I listen to yours?

I really don't mind scrutinising
Your emotional sores
But can you take my imperfections
If I tolerate yours?

If we're dealing in true confessions
I've got a few to share
Can we talk about my obsessions
When you come up for air?

Go on and tell me all the details
Like you're longing to do
But will you pay me some attention
If I listen to you?

I'll lend an ear to your adventures
On those sensual shores
But can we talk about *my* love life
When you've finished with yours?

UNDER-FAXED

His assets have been over-taxed
His latest dream has just been axed
He's trying hard to look relaxed
He's over-sexed and under-faxed

FILM CRITIC

There were bits of it I rather liked
But most of it I hated
The movie was like life itself –
Vastly overrated!

DEEPLY SHALLOW

I'M looking for a meaningless relationship
With a deeply shallow man
Passion with its awful fascination skip
That isn't in my plan

I'm looking for some small talk of the smallest kind
And a nice lighthearted fuck
I hope it's nothing serious you have in mind
If so, you're out of luck

Romance is off the menu
True love was yesterday
And if you seek commitment
The answer is – no way

I just can't take the sleepless nights and all that shit
I've escaped love's frying pan
Now I only want to mess around a little bit
With a deeply shallow
(This may be hard to swallow)
But I'm looking for a deeply shallow man

YOUR BORN-AGAIN FRIEND

YOUR born-again friend, how is he doing
Does faith uplift him when he's down
Does Jesus defend him from the screwing
That people get in tinsel town?

Although I only met him once
I've given him a lot of thought
Sometimes I think that his belief
Is like a germ that some have caught

Your born-again friend, does God protect him
From all the terrors we endure?
I may not agree, but I respect him
I wonder if he's still so sure

I'd like to know how well he copes
With all the tricks the system plays
And if he's really found a light
To guide him through these darkened days

We argued all day. I couldn't shake him
It was a stand-off in the end
But I wouldn't want the world to break him
Although I don't quite comprehend

Give my regards to
Your born-again friend

ABSENT FRIENDS

W<small>E</small> meet each other now and then
To drink and play 'remember when?'
A song begins, another ends
We always drink 'to absent friends'

To friends who showed us how to fly
Who made us laugh and made us cry
The tears we shed paid dividends
We owe a lot to absent friends

Here we are drinking under the stars
Showing our trophies, hiding our scars
Swapping confessions, trying to learn
If magic moments ever return

The lives we led in other days
Have left us lost in different ways
We wish that we could make amends
As we recall our absent friends

We've both been haunted by a ghost
But it was you I wanted most
Tonight let's take what fortune sends
    And maybe we'll forget
    Those absent friends

SURVIVOR'S SONG

WHEN I was young and fearless
I thought I'd live forever
I thought life was a party
And taking drugs was clever

And as for rules and morals
I didn't want or need 'em
I didn't care for safety
I wanted perfect freedom

Nobody stopped to count the cost
We travelled with the stars. It seems
That some survived and some were lost
I see their faces in my dreams

When I was young and reckless
I took a lot of chances
I toyed with self-destruction
Enjoyed narcotic trances

But now I count my blessings
Dear friends, and work, and bed
I've settled down (a little)
By rights I should be dead

On Location

To Boldly Go

To boldly go where no one sane has gone before
To land your ship upon a strange and smoky shore
To see new stars and learn about another race
To try to speak the language of another place

To boldly go although you're feeling ill at ease
To find new friends and leave behind old memories
To boldly go to parties arty and perverse
To navigate the oceans of the universe

Maybe when we get there
We'll know why we came
If our spaceship crashes
We've got ourselves to blame

To try new highs and giggle at some wicked words
To hear new sounds and meet exotic singing birds
To open up to someone you may never know
    To face your fear
    And boldly go

THE CALIFORNIA OF THE MIND

YOU'VE never been to California
But if you ever go there you will find
There really is no California
Like the California of the mind

There's fear and loathing in the air there
Stay home and let your fantasies unwind
'Cause when you get there, there's no 'there' there
Just armies of the blind leading the blind

The local beauties would all ignore you
The fads and follies would only bore you
The price of dreaming would simply floor you
On Malibu shore it's no fun any more

You won't find stardust on those beaches
The Gods and Goddesses have all resigned
So stay at home and pick your peaches
In the California of the mind

SUNSET BOULEVARD

Wipe your feet. Madame is waiting
Right this way, the fire's lit
Does the lady look familiar?
Long ago those eyes had 'it'
Stick around, Madame is lonely
She's not working any more
You can help her make her comeback
You're just what she's waiting for

Need new clothes? Madame will buy them
Feel this cashmere. Try these shoes
Get the best – the lady's paying
Go on – whatcha got to lose?
Go ahead, Madame adores you
You must take her in your arms
You've accepted all her presents
Now embrace her ageing charms

She'll feed you wine and caviar
And take you riding in her car
She was the biggest star of all
Before the pictures got so small

You walked in with eyes wide open
After all, it wasn't rape
All she asks is your affection
Don't you know you can't escape?
You can feel the noose grow tighter
Can't escape Madame's embrace
Can't escape from all those pictures
Of the lady's famous face

Just try to go
You won't get far
Nobody ever leaves a star

THROUGH THE
WINDOWS OF CARS

THROUGH the windows of cars
   My life flew by
I've seen rainbows and stars
Tattoo parlours and bars
Through the windows of cars

On the way to a dream
   I've seen it all
Fat cats chewing cigars
Beaches, brides and bazaars
Through the windows of cars

Cornfields and oceans and odd corners
Johnny-come-latelies and long-goners
Hotels, motels, rainy reflections
Future victims asking directions

Flashing by in the light
   My life flew by
Though it never seemed real
You were there at the wheel
And the world was ours
Through the windows of cars

Down the Road

Footfalls echo in the memory
Down the road we did not take
Toward the door we never opened
And the love we could not make

Shadows flicker in the memory
Of a clearing in the wood
Where we heard some spirit whisper
But we never understood

Between one dream and another
    The days run by
We spoil one scheme or the other
    And wonder why

Some believe it's all been written
Every move and every break
Every twist and every turning
Every tremble of the lake

Maybe when the dreams are over
One fine morning we'll awake
Hand in hand at last and singing
Down the road we did not take